The Story of A

A. is the pseudonym of a perfectly ordinary American who showed no signs of talent or greatness until he was over forty-five. Born in a modest mansion in the Westchester countryside, he lived through the normal childhood that any member of the family of an average steel magnate might have.

Life was hard in those days. He was only thirteen when his Cadillac was sold and his chauffeur had to take him to school piggyback.

At Groton and at Harvard, he experienced the obscure life of the average student. Except for a varsity letter in football and a Rhodes scholarship, there is virtually nothing worth mentioning. He obtained the routine Ph.D. in theoretical physics one would expect and began life at the bottom of the ladder in his father's steel company as fifth vice-president.

With women, A. was an utter failure. Six feet one inch tall, with curly brown hair, a bronzed complexion, a whimsical smile, regular features, broad shoulders, flat abdomen and narrow hips, there was nothing in him to attract the fair sex. Other than three or four dates on weekends, and perhaps four or five during the week, he lived the life of an anchorite. Except for three marriages, to two show girls and a Miss America, he was an utter celibate.

It was on his forty-fifth birthday that his life changed. Youth, he realized, was gone, but in its place, a steel determination gripped him. He developed finesse, art, experience and, as an old man, he found love at last.

Now he wants to pass on his great secret to you!

The
Sensuous

Dirty Old Man

CAUTION:
THIS IS A HUMOROUS BOOK NOT CONNECTED
WITH THE AUTHOR OR PUBLISHER OF ANY OTHER BOOK
DEALING WITH SENSUOSITY.

By Dr. "A"

A SIGNET BOOK from
NEW AMERICAN LIBRARY
TIMES MIRROR

Library of Congress Catalog Card Number: 76-166180

JAMES BUCHANAN: from portrait by George P. A. Healy, The Corcoran Gallery of Art

WINSTON CHURCHILL: Keystone

CHARLES CURTIS: International

BENJAMIN FRANKLIN: courtesy of the New York Historical Society, New York City

OLIVER WENDELL HOLMES: National Photo

KING LEAR: Culver Pictures

JONATHAN SWIFT: courtesy of the Curators of the Bodleian Library

Thanks to the New York Public Library for providing prints of the remaining pictures

Published by arrangement with Walker and Company. The hardcover edition was published simultaneously in Canada by Fitzhenry & Whiteside, Limited, Toronto.

SIGNET, SIGNET CLASSICS, SIGNETTE, MENTOR and PLUME BOOKS are published by The New American Library, Inc., 1301 Avenue of the Americas, New York, New York 10019

FIRST PRINTING, JUNE, 1972

PRINTED IN THE UNITED STATES OF AMERICA

ADAM & EVE

THE
SENSUOUS
DIRTY
OLD MAN

BECOMING

AN

OLD

MAN

WHEN I WAS YOUNG, I SOMETIMES THOUGHT OF the possibility of becoming an old man. I wasn't overwhelmed at the prospect. The longer I thought about it the more I decided that being an old man wasn't for me.

For others, maybe. For people who liked being gray, or bald (or both) it had its advantages. For people who were crazy about creaking joints it was something to look forward to. For me, however, who was young, gay, vibrant and debonair, it was a big nothing.

So I decided never to be an old man. I decided never to reach forty.

A friend of mine accomplished that task. He did so in a very simple and straightforward manner. He died at thirty-six.

This shook me. I must admit I had not thought it through. I sat down and began thinking. Carefully I counted on my fingers and worked up the line of years. In order not to reach forty, one had to die at the age of no more than thirty-nine. That's the way it worked out.

Don't think I just seized that figure out of the air. I worked it out a dozen times in a dozen different ways. Take my word for it. Unless you die at thirty-nine (or before that, if you're in a hurry), you're going to turn forty.

What's more, unless you die at forty-nine (or before), you're going to turn fifty. And unless you die at fifty-nine (or before), you're—

I'll leave it to you at this point. Assuming you took math in college, you can carry on from there. Only the simplest of analytical geometry is required.

So let's summarize. You have a clear choice of two alternatives. You can either die young, or you can grow old.

Naturally, if you have made up your mind to die, you will not be interested in what is going to happen to you when you are old and you may not want to pay the trivial sum required to buy this book. On the other hand, even if you will stay young until your premature demise, you may be curious about the way your father has been behaving lately, so buy it anyway. Leafing through the pages in the bookstore—as you are doing—will bring you bad luck and you will be hit by a truck at the first intersection you try to cross. So pay your money; it's friendly advice.

If, on the other hand, you have decided not to die young (and congratulations on a wise decision), then you must certainly buy this book, for in it you will learn how to make the most of old age. You will find in it how to have the kind of love you only dared dream about when you were young. Whatever price you pay for the book, it will be worth it.

The question arises, of course, as to what a woman should do. Suppose, for instance, a young lady were to pick up this book in search of material of social significance (something that is instantly indicated by the word "sensuous" in the title). It is reasonable to suspect that she might pause and ask herself, "Will I ever grow to be an old man?"

It is a difficult question and deserves a thoughtful answer. If the girl persists in living, she will surely grow old, but there is very little chance that she will grow to be an old man. A close examination of actuarial tables put out by the life insurance companies makes it nearly certain that she will grow to be an old woman, which is a different thing.

Ought she then *not* read this book?

On one condition only. Provided she has never met a dirty old man and expects never to do so in the future.

Mind you, it is quite possible for a girl to go through life without meeting a dirty old man. To give you a simple example— Suppose a girl is marooned on a desert island at birth, an island on which no other human being exists, and remains there the rest of her life. She will never meet a dirty old man. If a copy of this book were to wash up on the shore of such an island, she would be wasting money if she were to pay for it.*

If we consider women who have not had the fortunate experience of being marooned for life on a desert island, the situation is altered. We can be certain that they have had occasion to meet a dirty old man. In fact, those women whose delightful charms have matured, ripened and mellowed to the point of middle age (or perhaps "late youth" is a better term) would scarcely have a chance to meet anyone else.

Young men—green, gawky, loutish—have eyes only for young women. Dirty old men, however, have eyes for whatever they happen to be looking at. Any matron who longs for the days when she had to worry about masculine impertinence had better rely on the dirty old man.

Or, as Sir Walter Scott once said, musing on this very point—

---

*That is, if she expected useful information out of it. On the other hand, the mere chance of immersing oneself in the author's pleasant writing style would be well worth the small sum paid out.

SIR WALTER SCOTT

Breathes there a dame, with hope so dead,
Who never to herself has said,
  "I want my own, my dirty man."
Whose heart within her ne'er hath burned
As home her footsteps she hath turned
  Still seeking one wherever she can.*

Naturally, then the mature woman should buy this book. To put it briefly, everyone should.

---

*All quotations in this book are given from memory. Fortunately I have a pretty near photographic memory—I can remember anything that is pretty near a photograph—so you may rely on the quotations being absolutely accurate except for an occasional word or two that don't count.

BECOMING

A DIRTY

OLD

MAN

WHEN I WAS YOUNG I CAME ACROSS A BEAUTIFUL line of poetry that went:

> In the spring, a young man's fancy lightly
> turns to thoughts of love.*

When I was young, I naturally thought that the important word in the line was "young." Only a young man's fancy, I thought, would turn to love.

*This comes from "Locksley Hall" by Alfred, Lord Tennyson. Do not, however, be misled by this line into racing to get the poem in the hope that it will contain a great deal of social significance. It is, you will be sorry to hear, completely clean.

ALFRED, LORD TENNYSON

He was strong, he was muscular, he was lissome (whatever that means) and he could turn "lightly" —skipping and prancing.

An old man, whose feet hurt him, I reasoned, couldn't turn "lightly" to anything.

Once I started speculating about the coming of age, thoughts of this line depressed me. Oh, how sorrowful it was to grow old and have to abandon all "thoughts of love." Imagine growing old and no longer thinking about hips and bosoms and all the other intellectual and socially significant things one finds on the beach and in the girlie magazines.

But then I discovered something that has turned my life to gold. Let me share it with you.

The important word in that line of poetry is "spring."*

Love is, after all, a seasonal thing with the young. Once a year, sometime in May, the young man manages to pump up enough hormonal pressure to wink at a girl. For the rest of the year, it

---

*It is doubtful if Lord Tennyson himself ever realized this. He lived to be eighty-three years old without ever crossing the threshold of dirtyhood. One finds it easy to believe that not once after the age of forty did he hold a young girl's hand in his and say, looking into her eyes soulfully, "Call me Alfie, dear."

PRIME MINISTER WILLIAM E.
GLADSTONE

all goes into football or handball or beer parties or other activities with no trace of social significance about them.

As a man grows old, however, he puts away childish things. He begins to sort out the essentials from the nonessentials. By carefully husbanding his resources, he finds that he can tackle the matter of girls at any time.

The line of poetry should read:

> In the spring, a young man's fancy lightly
> turns to thoughts of what
> The older man, throughout the year, has
> never even once forgot.

Is this true of all old men? No, of course not. I mentioned Tennyson before as a fellow who developed from a rather unpromising youth into the gray limbo of the type of person called "a clean old man."*

Nor is Tennyson the only one. Prime Minister William E. Gladstone of Great Britain was a clean old man. So were President of the United States

---

*This is not something to sneer at, or shudder away from. The clean old man is neither to be shunned nor censured. He is to be *helped*. It is not a sin but a sickness, not a crime but a psychiatric problem.

PRESIDENT JAMES BUCHANAN

James Buchanan and the American statesman William Jennings Bryan.

There is little left for such clean old men to do. When not sleeping through the sermon in church on Sunday, they are forced to spend their time in the unrewarding pursuit of money and power. The English poet, William Wordsworth, himself a clean old man, saw this coming and when only thirty-six years of age, wrote, in an agony of apprehension, the immortal lines—

> The world is too much with us; late and soon,
> Getting and spending, we lay waste our powers:
> Little we see in Nature that is ours.

In fact, what is more dreadful still is that we live in an age where every effort is made to hold up to our admiration those who have willingly (or unwillingly, perhaps) turned into clean old men while still in their teens. Billy Graham leaps to the mind, for instance, and, if we are not careful, so does President Richard M. Nixon.

We must fight this. We must stop laying waste our powers and must get back to Nature—as Wordsworth advises.

WILLIAM WORDSWORTH

We must not be taken in by the myth of youth, the unending propaganda to the effect that young men are younger than old men; that they are better looking; that they are slimmer, stronger and more athletic; that they can hold a girl in more romantic fashion and speak more sweetly.

Nonsense! Pure balderdash put out by a secret organization of clean old men whose design it is to conquer the world and who use the unwitting young as fronts and dupes.

The fact of the matter is that young men lack skill and experience and are very likely to approach a girl as though she were a sack of wheat. It is the old man—suave, debonair, maturely charming—who knows exactly what to do and how to do it, and is therefore better at it.

In fact, once when I imprinted on a young lady's lips a chaste and fatherly kiss for about five minutes, I stopped and said, sorrowfully, "Wouldn't you rather be kissed by a twenty-one-year-old boy?"

She frowned and said, "Of course not. If you'd ever been kissed by a twenty-one-year-old boy*

*Oddly enough, I haven't.

you'd know better than to ask."

Remember that. In any direct competition, the old man is bound to win and the young man knows it. What, then, is the young man's defense? He calls names. He speaks of a "dirty old man."

He intends it as an insult, at least at the start.

Very few people know this. Very few people are aware of the fact that in the beginning the proud and glorious phrase "dirty old man" was actually meant as derision.

The very phrase, originated as it was by young men, is a standing testimonial to the ignorance of the same young men. Sex *is* dirty—if you do it right. Young men don't know how to do it right, so they stay clean. Some old men never learn how and they stay clean, too.

But unless you have the ambition to retreat into dull hopelessness, don't you do it. Don't be bashful with the ladies while young and retreat altogether as you grow older. Grow bolder with the years; advance, advance.

Be a dirty old man and be proud of it.

That's the way Robert Browning felt. Unlike William Wordsworth, who mourned the future,

Browning gloried in it. He said—

> Grow old along with me!
> The best is yet to be,
> The last of life, for which the first was made.

One word of warning, though. Sometimes the word "dirty" is confused with a very similar word "dirty" which means "grimy." It is true that if an old man does not bathe meticulously, he becomes a dirty old man, but not in the meaning of the phrase as used in this book. In order to distinguish between the two words, I will spell the word in capitals when it indicates grimy. Thus, Charles II of Great Britain was a gloriously dirty old man. His grandfather, James I, on the other hand, was a DIRTY old man.

ROBERT BROWNING

BECOMING A

SENSUOUS

DIRTY

OLD MAN

NATURALLY, THERE IS NO POINT IN BEING A DIRTY
old man and keeping it a secret. It is probably not
even good for your health.

Consider Aaron Burr, for instance. He was
once vice-president of the United States, and was
a convinced and dedicated dirty old man. He lived
to be eighty and flaunted his dirtdom to the end.
Alexander Hamilton, on the other hand, while a
dirty old man, too, kept it a secret and undoubtedly developed a nervous tremor in consequence. In
1804, Aaron Burr and Alexander Hamilton had a
duel. In view of Hamilton's nervousness, developed over long years of hoping no one would no-

AARON BURR

ALEXANDER HAMILTON

tice he was a dirty old man, he missed. Burr did not. There is a moral here.

Benjamin Franklin was a dirty old man, too, who made no secret of it and who reached the pinnacle of fame and public esteem. What's more, he lived to be eighty-four. President Warren G. Harding, however, was a dirty old man who strove to seem clean and he died at fifty-seven. Is it coincidence that Harding is one of the least regarded of our presidents?

I could go on and on, but let us get away from history and consider you.

Let us imagine that you are a dirty old man but are dedicated to keeping it a secret because you are a bank vice-president and are interested in exuding an odor of sanctity so that no one will notice, until it is too late, that you are preparing to abscond.

Now a lovely girl walks past you with a dress whose neckline is generously loose and under which there is clearly and obviously no bra. What do you do?

What you do is roll your eyes briefly in their sockets with the eyelashes lowered so that no one

BENJAMIN FRANKLIN

PRESIDENT WARREN G. HARDING

will see what you are doing. The result? You don't see anything at all, except perhaps for one flash of quiver that is far more upsetting than sating.

And what is the girl's reaction? She sees that flicker of eye even if no one else does (since she's watching for it) and despises you as a rotten little coward. You see that look of contempt in her eye (for it goes through you like an icepick) and your self-esteem is shattered. Indeed, there is a very good chance that the girl will instantly realize that a man who would look at her with so miserably sidelong a glance is a man who would abscond with every cent of the bank's property and she will inform on you at once.

But suppose you are not only a dirty old man, but are proud of it, too, and suppose the same girl walks by in the same condition. Now it is possible to be joyous and open. You can emit a melodious whistle or a snort of pleasure. You can stare openly. You can walk over to get a closer view. You can address the girl in friendly fashion.

And how does the girl react? Why she is pleased that she has created such an obvious stir in a gentleman of such substantial and prosperous appearance. She realizes that you agree with her own opinion of herself and this can't help but impress her with the excellence of your taste.

Seeing in you a person whom she can respect, she will think, "What a nice, gentlemanly old man," and will smile at you. From that to a friendly word or two is but a step, and from that to a pat on the cheek or some slight pressure on the upper arm is but another.

Your own self-esteem will shoot up and if you are the vice-president of a bank, you will be so buoyed up by all this that you will go right to your office and put back all the money. This is only one example of many I can cite in which being an open and honest dirty old man is an enormous aid to public morality.

And remember, without being openly a dirty old man, you can never practice your craft; you can never learn to refine and sharpen your technique; you can, in short, never learn to be a *sensuous* dirty old man.

But if you are dirty *and* open, you will become sensuous, and this book is intended to help you in achieving this glorious aim.

AT WHAT AGE
CAN ONE
BECOME A
DIRTY OLD MAN?

NATURALLY, AS THE ADVANTAGES OF DIRTY-OLD-manship become apparent, youth will aspire to its ecstasies at as early an age as possible. Just as some young men sink into the epicene apathy of clean-old-manhood at sixteen, so others, with far more pith and marrow, rise to the energy of dirty-old-mandom.

But to advance, to climb, to aspire, is not easy. Any youngster can become a clean old man. It requires nothing more than nothingness to do so. To become a dirty old man takes more; it takes the finest spirit man can show.

It was once said of me that I had been a dirty

old man from the age of fifteen, but perhaps that is an exaggeration.

The difficulties a teen-ager must overcome in scaling the peak of dirtiness are enormous. The teen-ager lacks the necessary experience, the cachet, the view of womanhood. He is, in short, frightened, insecure, unsure.

This is nothing to be unduly distressed over. Of all the diseases of mankind, that one from which one most surely recovers is youth. The recovery is, however, agonizingly slow in some cases and it can, within limits, be hastened. One can encourage the oncoming of ripeness, if not chronologically, then at least psychologically. Remember this important lesson: To *act* like a dirty old man is to *be* a dirty old man.

If, therefore, you read this book carefully and learn how to act like one, you will be one even if you are fairly young.

Remember, too, that the essence of a dirty old man is the inner spirit. The outer appearance is secondary. Many a young man can place a dirty leer on his cherubic countenance, while many another, already lined with approaching age, cannot.

A young man came to me once, sobbing. It had occurred to him that he might dye his beard a speckled gray so as to give himself the appearance of age and participate in the delights of being a dirty old man. After manful attempts, however, he had failed to grow a beard.

I placed my hand on his shoulder and responded with the beautiful words of Charles Kingsley:

> Think old, sweet youth, and let who will be
> bearded.

Last time I saw him he was staring at girls' legs in the subway. The barest beginnings, of course, but he was happy. As far as dirty-old-manhood was concerned, he was quite obviously trying it on for thighs.

CHARLES KINGSLEY

HOW LONG

CAN ONE

STAY

A DIRTY

OLD MAN?

I MUST BE FRANK WITH YOU. THIS BOOK WOULD BE worthless to you if I were not. The fact is that one can't stay a dirty old man forever and you will have to face that fact steadily and unafraid.

You can be a dirty old man only as long as you live. Once you die, it's over.

Oliver Wendell Holmes, the great Supreme Court Justice, in his last years (he lived to be ninety-four), was walking down Pennsylvania Avenue with a friend, when a pretty girl passed. As all dirty old men must, especially when the dignity

OLIVER WENDELL HOLMES

of the Supreme Court is at stake, Holmes turned to look after her. Having done so, he sighed and said to his friend, "Ah, George, what wouldn't I give to be seventy-five again?"

This is an excellent object-lesson in how even the greatest and most highly placed among us may go wrong. What Holmes was hankering for was youth; he wanted to be a boy of seventy-five again, and why? Did he plan to approach the girl? To sweep her off her feet with his youthful verve and charm? To lure her on with promises of champagne and roses? To trap her in some hotel room?

Imagine the spate of trouble that would have created. There would have been a veritable flood of hard feelings on the bench. Justice Louis D. Brandeis would have demanded to know why he himself had not received an introduction. President Herbert Hoover would have asked if she had a friend. And what of Mrs. Holmes, a spry old lady, perfectly capable of raising havoc with all concerned. Think of the turmoil in Washington.

Instead, by the mere act of turning around, Holmes had, despite his noble nonagenarianism,

JUSTICE LOUIS D. BRANDEIS

acted reasonably well the high-minded part of dirty old man. The story does not tell whether he emitted a throaty chuckle as he did so, or pounded his cane on the sidewalk, or even (by placing one hand on his cane and the other on his friend's shoulder) kicked his heels in the air. All these would have added sophistication to his actions and would have been well within the bounds of his physical capacity. Since I am a great admirer of Holmes and a believer in his sensuosity, I cannot help but feel that he did all three.

In doing so, Holmes proved (even though he himself may have missed the point) that any man, whatever his age, provided only that he can move his eyes and breathe, can be a dirty old man.

—And the story has a happy ending. Because Holmes, despite his foolish wish for youth, acted the dirty old man with dignity and efficiency, all Washington was heartened. Justice Brandeis merely said to Justice Benjamin Cardozo, "Let me tell you about the chick I saw last week—" and the rest died away in a sibilant whisper.

As for President Hoover, who was in his fifties at the time, he is reported to have said to Vice-

JUDGE BENJAMIN N. CARDOZO

President Charles Curtis, when the news of Holmes's cogent behavior reached him, "Charlie, Charlie, what wouldn't I give to be ninety?" (He made it, too—with two months to spare.)

VICE-PRESIDENT CHARLES CURTIS

USE

YOUR

EYES!

THERE ARE MANY THEORIES AS TO THE NATURE OF the prime tool of the dirty old man. There are those who hold out for a cane, others for thick eyeglasses or a ragged mustache, a long coat, or some other article of clothing. Some, in considering what the prime tool might be, advance the most ridiculous suggestions imaginable.

The answer is so simple, however, that one wonders why there is any doubt or dispute. It is his eyes!

Imagine, for a moment, that you are a dirty old man with your eyes closed. (If you *are* a dirty old man, it is child's play to imagine this.)

Suppose, next, that you are surrounded by lovely
ladies. What can you do with your eyes closed?
You might hear the pitter-patter of high heels, be
tantalized by the rustle of dresses, by the fragrant
whiff of perfume. You might be able to trip one
of the delightful creatures by a lucky thrust of
your cane, if you carry one, or brush against one
with your overcoat (or your mustache if you'd
rather, though that's a more difficult target).

But what a world of loveliness breaks upon
your delighted self as soon as you open your eyes.
There are the ladies, visible in large quantity and
in all their detail.

Of course, the value of the eyes depends on their
being used.

That is so simple a matter you would imagine
that there could be no quarrel with it, and yet how
many folksayings seem to contradict this obvious
fact. Consider the odium in which old Thomas the
Tailor is held for an injudicious act of his involving
his eyes.

Thomas was a tailor in eleventh-century Coven-
try, at a time when Lady Godiva for some reason
best known to herself decided to ride through the

town on a horse, naked. (Herself naked, not the horse—though actually the horse wasn't wearing much either.) All the townsmen rushed indoors at once, firmly determined not to look. But Thomas, overcome by curiosity, bored a small hole in the shutter of his shop and peeped. He was instantly struck blind, and small wonder, since Godiva must have been a pretty marrow-freezing sight if the lusty inhabitants of an eleventh-century English town refused to look at her.

Thomas went down in history as "Peeping Tom" and his story has been used as an object-lesson against old men looking at girls.

But the object-lesson is distorted. Surely it should be plain to the veriest dunce that the danger lies in *peeping*. Viewed that way, the lesson is a valuable one.

Don't peep at girls—STARE!

The worst of the antioptic propaganda is inflicted on innocent childhood. Children are indoctrinated from their very earliest years with such phrases as: "Close your eyes, sweetie-pie, and you'll get a surprise."

This association of closed eyes and surprises

lasts all life long in some cases, but what is the surprise you get when you close your eyes? Just this: It is when you close your eyes that a girl in hot pants passes. And what do you get in return for those closed eyes and that missed chance—a crummy piece of candy, most likely. That may sound like a good exchange to an infant or a glutton, but not to an old man of spirit.

As a result of youthful training and literary mischief, too many old men have never learned to use their eyes.

I'll give you an example. On the TV program, "Candid Camera," movies were taken of what happened when a girl dressed in a scanty bikini walked into a hardware store to buy a pint of nails and a loaf of electric wiring. She was a shapely wench of the kind that would simply fill a hardware store with hard ware.

In the store were ordinary customers, also, including men of mature years, who, under better conditions of upbringing, might well have been dirty old men of decency.

What do you suppose these men did? Nothing. They looked away, blushing so hard that my

---

black-and-white set broke into embarrassed color. Occasionally, as in the case of the banker I mentioned earlier, one of them would flick his eyes to one side in an attempt to get an optical whiff of beauty.

Over and over again the sequence was taken at different times and at different stores. Always the same. Always the painful unawareness and the occasional flick of eyes.

Pretending to be unaware of the young lady, mind you, is not only a negation of whatever miserable manhood the negating person may aspire to, but is a foul and ungentlemanly insult to the young lady. Did you ever think of that?

Well, think of it.

Here's a charming young lady, rose-pink with youth and utterly happy in her charming virginity, struggling with squeals of delight into an upper and lower garment carefully fitted by her proud mamma into an exact 1.5 sizes too small. She is then sent off to the hardware store, bashfully aware that she is pretty, and overlapping in all directions, and simply waiting for someone to take notice of her so that she might dimple and curtsy in appreciation.

And what happens? The clods don't look at her but find themselves overwhelmingly interested in samples of wall-sockets. What is that but a clear indication that the clods would rather plug into the wall-socket, so to speak, than into the young lady.

The poor thing probably cried her eyes out— to say nothing of the broken heart of the gray-haired mother.

As for the eye-flickering, that is worse yet. I have mentioned it in connection with the banker, but let us now go into greater detail.

First, the young lady sees it, of course, and considers you (as I said before) a contemptible coward. There is worse, however. If she is particularly inexperienced, she will interpret the quick look away as signifying that even the most evanescent view of her body must be sickening. To cause such a feeling to rise in the breast of a young girl is clearly the act of a miserable cad—all the more so since the feeling, in view of the style of dress being considered, is more than ordinarily visible.

Second, you are yourself cheated. There is a momentary glimpse of maidenly quiver, a quick impression of the gentle lift of soft flesh. That is no good. That is worse than useless. It merely drives home to you, you miserable hobbledehoy, that you are not only a coward but that you don't even have the common decency to be a thorough-going coward and not look at all.

Third, it is bad for the eyes. Twists like that produce small stretchings and tearings of the eyeball muscles that gradually unfit them for their work. It also makes the eyes sore, which is why Jonathan Swift coined a phrase once by saying, when Stella passed him in dishabille, "Gee, kid, you sure are a sight for sore eyes!"

Well, then, what should a person do when a bikini-clad damsel takes her place at one's side? Isn't it obvious? One should look.

If you doubt my word, take that of Robert Burns, the great Scots poet who, before dying at the age of thirty-seven, had made an enviable mark as a dirty old man at a remarkably early age. He said, if memory serves—

> Oh, wad some power the giftie gie us
> To see a lass as others see us!
> It would frae mony a blunder free us.
>   An' foolish notion.

JONATHAN SWIFT

It is obvious from these lines Burns considered that to "see a lass" was a direct way of freeing one-self from blunders and from the foolish notions that one ought not to look. And let me tell you, Robert Burns knew what he was talking about.

ROBERT BURNS

VARIATIONS IN EYE USE

MERELY TO STARE IS CRUDE. THE YOUNG LADY CAN never be sure if it is a stare of admiration (which would please her) or one of surprise and disapproval (which very likely wouldn't please her—and would most certainly offend her mother). It is only reasonable, therefore, that you add to the stare something that would indicate pleasure. These addenda can be divided into two classes: silent and audible.

The silent method involves some gesture bespeaking due appreciation of the vision of loveliness before you—something that would, if placed in words, be the equivalent of—

You walk in beauty, like the night, kid,

Of cloudless climes and starry skies;
And all that's best of dark and bright, baby,
Meet in your aspect and your eyes.

As a matter of historical fact, Lord Byron once said something very much like this to a damsel in Pisa who unfortunately couldn't understand English and pretended to misconstrue Byron's Italian. A bottle of Chianti and an English bank note fluttered from the fingers made everything clear—which shows the occasional advantage of the silent method over the audible.*

Do not try to imitate Byron by obtaining a bottle of Chianti and an English bank note. Times have changed. Neither, especially the latter, is as effective as it once was. Besides, Byron was an advanced student whose work is not to be imitated by the beginner.

Besides, so much can be done so simply. You might simply roll the eyes, or open them widely, or raise and lower the eyebrows rapidly, or shake the head slowly from side to side, or slowly lick the lips or even merely grin. Each of these is a polite but expressive indication that the girl in the

---

*It must be remembered that Lord Byron was an extraordinarily gifted individual who, by sheer instinct, was a dirty old man from earliest youth.

LORD BYRON

bikini looks like a clean, healthy and virtuous
young lady, and this can only be gratifying to all
concerned.

Is there any way of indicating which of these
suggestions, for instance, is best for the purpose?
There is no definite answer, for a great deal depends on the shape of your face, the color of your
eyes, the curve of your eyebrows.

Some authorities, such as Reuben David in his
famous treatise, *What You Have Always Asked
About Sex (But Didn't Really Want to Know)* ad-
vocate practicing before the mirror. He describes
these as "sensual exercises."

Nonsense, it is very easy to demonstrate that
such practice leads only to self-consciousness. Besides, you are no judge of your own stare; it is not
intended to please you, but a young lady, and you
are not a young lady. (If you are in any doubt on
this vital matter, consult a gynecologist at once.)

No, far better to follow instinct. Remember,
Mother Nature is interested in the matter. She has
spent two or three billion years in evolving the
dirty old man and you must learn to let those bil-
lions of years of evolution work for you. Instinct

will lead you aright and a little bit of trial and error won't hurt, either.

There is the case, for instance, of the man who, on sighting an interesting young lady, quite inadvertently wiggled his ears. The effect was to have the young lady stare back in fascination and hold whatever pose it was that had first attracted his attention. There were even times, he tells me, where there was a most desirable side-effect: The young lady nudged a friend of hers who also turned and looked, holding a pose.

But enough of silence. Let us go on to audible adjuncts to staring.

Here again there is much room for individual variation. There is the startled gasp; the sharp intake of breath; the snort; the low hum; or any combination of these, with or without a gesture. There may even be an articulation of syllable, such as "Wow!" or, for the more loquacious, "Oh, boy!"

I strongly recommend deliberate variation in this respect. You may hear from a number of "authorities" that there is only one proper way of accompanying a smile; a respectful hand upon the heart, perhaps, combined with a slight bow. Such beliefs arose in seventeenth-century France, a stylized period, and have nothing to do with the natural urges of dirtykind. Intense psychological studies carried out in recent decades have made it quite clear that *any* device, however interesting and effective in itself, loses that interest and effect if repeated too often and too predictably. It is the new and unexpected that produces the best response.

This does not mean that you should never repeat, or that you should go far afield in the endless search for novelty. Try variations, but from a tried armory.

If you are not self-assured in your role as a dirty old man, you have probably listened to others in bars and locker rooms telling of their experiences. They have described the girls passing by on the streets and then, in a low voice, with everyone else listening in rapt fashion, told you of their great deeds—how they shook one hand violently and said, "Va-va-va-VOOM" or "Oskie-wow-wow-mamma-MEEah." You probably listened enviously and wondered why it was *you* couldn't display such virility.

Don't fall for it! Those who talk in this fashion usually pick up such phrases from pornographic books, which are filled with faulty psychology.

The chances are if you catch these big-mouths in action, you will find that at the appearance of a girl it is all they can do to smile. The use of "Va-va-va-VOOM," or any other set of nonsense syllables, requires so much inner preparation, so much mumbling under the breath to make sure you have the intonation right, that the girl approaches, passes and is gone before you can get it out—unless, of course, you are a person who has practiced strenuously for many years, and by then you will undoubtedly have far more effective routines.

On the whole, it is better to eschew complications. A simple "Wow" in sufficiently heartfelt manner, or even a snort, will do much better.

If you are fortunate enough to carry a cane, either rap it sharply on the ground as the young lady approaches or, using it as a pivot, slowly turn as she passes. This is an extremely effective course of action which, when properly carried through, gains the admiration of one and all. The "cane-pivot" carries with it, however, the chance of what is technically known as "slippage." Beware of that. Falling down is not only painful but ruins the effect.*

In general, if there is a single rule to remember it is that of simplicity. The simple approach, perfectly carried through, is much more effective than something that is elaborate, but shaky.

---

*There is some argument about this. I know a man who claims that he falls down in such a way that the young lady quickly runs to help him up and that he can occupy five minutes at least in being so helped. However, I have not seen this with my own eyes.

THE
LEER

IN ALL THE REALM OF DIRTY-OLD-MANDOM, THERE is nothing on which so much misinformation is prevalent as on the leer.

To most people a leer is the very opposite of a mere stare. It is argued that the stare itself is ineffective; that it exists outside the world of the dirty-old-man; that people stare for all kinds of reasons.

This is true enough, for there is the haughty stare, the displeased stare, the astonished stare. There are stares delivered by old ladies or by policemen—or that most poisonous stare of all, the stare of the author who is asked for revisions. These are indeed examples of "empty stares" with no important content.

Opposed to the mere stare, in popular mythology, is the leer. The leer always has content, for it has only one meaning: salacious admiration.

The very word "salacious" seems admirably fitted to the old man's art, for it is from a Latin phrase meaning "given to leaping" and indicates that a girl who gets a leer of salacious admiration will leap with joy—and it is to be admitted that those old Romans knew a thing or two. Julius Caesar was probably the most prominent of all the dirty old men who ever wore a toga, easily outstripping Mark Antony, for all the latter's reputation. Indeed, as the old English saying has it:

> When Caesar leered and Cleo ran,
> Who was then the dirty old man?*

With all this favorable propaganda for leers

*There is a version of this romantic old saying which is frequently quoted and which goes: *When Adam delved and Eve span, Who was then the gentleman?* This version is credited to someone with the improbable name of John Ball. One can see how this corruption came into use, for "delved" means "dug," so that, in modern parlance, Adam "dug" Eve, which would seem likely, and throughout English history, what the English called a "gentleman" was very much like what we would call "a dirty old man." The only real puzzle is Adam and Eve, since they, whoever they were, were certainly not Roman.

MARC ANTONY

(even to the point where it has become a favorite cliché to say, "The dirty old man leered at the girl"), there are few people who can actually describe what a leer is.

The answer may surprise you. The leer is the look out of the corner of the eye that I mentioned scornfully on two different occasions earlier in the book.

If you don't believe me, look it up in the dictionary.

This may puzzle you. If the leer is merely a side-wise glance, which I have stigmatized as not only worthless, but actually harmful, how has it come about that it is so highly regarded?

The difference, you see, is between the dictionary's opinion of what "leer" means and the actual use of the word. After all, the dictionary, you must understand, is a largely useless volume intended to serve as a monument to the language as used in the previous century. Taken literally as a guide to present-day usage it is not only misleading, it can bring about assault and battery.

Thus, the dictionary defines "gay" as "excited with merriment." It is therefore only necessary to approach some huge hulk of a fellow who is excited with merriment and say, "You're gay, aren't you?" and see what happens to you!*

So ask not what Webster is saying to the American public, ask rather what the American public is saying to Webster. (I once said this to a speechwriter for a senator from Massachusetts in a letter I wrote him and he used it later in a speech—but of course he got it all twisted.)

The fact is that, to the general public, a "leer" is defined as a "dirty smile." If this is the definition then a leer is rightly the strongest weapon in the long-distance armory of the dirty old man. What better activity for a dirty old man than a dirty old smile. And it is not our generation alone that thinks so. Shakespeare, four and a half centuries ago centered an entire play about it.**

And how does one make a smile dirty? Why pre-

---

*If he isn't gay, he is very likely to fell you to the ground with a mighty blow. If he *is*, the consequences to you may be even more appalling.

**"King Leer" of course. I'm amazed you should ask. And Leonardo da Vinci painted the "Mona Leersa" to celebrate it, though the name of the picture is so frequently misspelled that the point is lost.

KING LEAR

cisely in the manner I described in the preceding chapter. By rolling the eyes, raising the eyebrows, clicking the tongue, uttering a "Wow" and so on.

In short, what I have been talking about for pages and pages is the leer as practiced by dirty old men, if not as defined in the dictionary.

WHAT DO

YOU

LEER AT?

AT GIRLS, DO YOU SAY? TO BE SURE, BUT THAT IS just the beginning.

Girls represent a vast area, stretching from the crown of the upsweep hairdo to the tip of the big toe, from the bulge of the left hip to that of the right shoulder, from the jutting outthrust of the frontal breastworks to the curving caboose of the rear balcony.

No portion of that area, no square inch, is without its special delight, but to allow the leer to wander aimlessly, first here, then there, is the mark of the irresolute child. No possible respect can be held for such a restlessly wandering eye by any woman, especially since she is left unsure, by such pusillanimous behavior, as to which aspect of herself is most worthy of the admiration of an experienced man.

You ought therefore choose certain restricted and particularly desirable areas at which to leer. In such matters, it is best to be guided by the young lady herself. She knows what she wants you to look at, so regard her closely.

What is her make-up telling you? What is that carefully unbuttoned button whispering? (Well, get closer and listen.) What is that well-trained gap murmuring?

Before World War I, the problem was perhaps not as great as it is now. Women were well-swathed and it was with the greatest difficulty that one could point out something at which one might look. As the well-known ballad puts it:

> In olden days, 'twas simply shocking
> To have to leer at a glimpse of stocking

Nowadays, however, "anything goes." Much less is left to the imagination, and the rewards of the leer are enormous. With it, of course (no rights without their duties), is the responsibility of directing the leer among the many possible directions.

The most obvious area is that which we learned to love in babyhood. Even in Victorian times, there were dresses with astonishing décolletage, or, to use the French expression, "cut way down in front." These, however, were seen only at the fancier social occasions, which were open only to the upper classes. While the men of the upper classes labored nobly at being dirty old men, contemporary Americans feel—and rightly—that dirtyhood is the birthright of all men, however lowly.

In our more democratic society, therefore, any young lady from the highest-paid and haughtiest housemaid right down to the most lowly and submissive suburban housewife has the full permission to display as much of her frontal equipment as she dares at any time she chooses.

Many people regard the matter of mammary display as a frontal attack on our standards of morality. Sometimes, I tend to agree with them. Many is the occasion on which I have looked down on low-cut dresses.

It is not, however, the business of the sensuous

dirty old man to uphold the standards of morality of American womanhood, however much his innate decency impels him to the task. It is rather his mission in life to come to the aid of suffering womanhood first, and worry about morality afterward, if at all.

Consider the dilemma of the young lady, for instance, who feels impelled to make known to the world at large the superlative properties of her sublaryngeal area. The fact that she does so is a tribute to her efforts to make America beautiful, for it has its drawbacks. It is 8 A.M. of a brisk spring morning and the temperature is 40° F. at the bus stop. In her eagerness to brighten the day, she has displayed a stretch of her chest to the elements.

Now do you suppose she *wants* to catch cold? Do you think she *intends* to come down with an attack of virulent goose-pimples that may (just barely may) fester? No, she is merely following the golden rule which, in case you have forgotten, goes, as nearly as I can recall it: Do unto others as others would like to have you do unto them.

Is this noble and selfless girl to be ignored? Is

she to be allowed to cough herself into pitiful pneumonia with no leer to light the path to the hospital cot? Never. Surely not while America boasts her squads of earnest dirty old men.

If you are one and should spy a damsel of this sort, approach and, for the sake of decency and humanity, leer. Let there be no mistake about what it is you are leering at. Bend your eyes boldly at the dressline; chuckle throatily; snort and make clicking noises with your tongue. In short, offer the young lady your respectful attention and she will walk past you gratefully, wheezing a bit, but warmed by your respectful attention to the point where she may escape pneumonia after all.

Nor are esoteric leers to be ignored. The sleeveless dress has long made the axillary area (or, to use the politer medical term, "armpit") a place to be considered with some respect. It may be ignored in the romantic love story, disregarded in the popular love song and even omitted as a subject for discussion in the racier sermons delivered on Sunday mornings, but the sight of a young lady properly semiclothed, hanging onto a strap in the subway on a hot summer day, will keep an old man glued to his seat far past his proper stop.

The miniskirt offers countless opportunities for the long, slow leer, whether viewed from fore or aft and needs scarcely any direction. The rank beginner knows where to sit, how to look and when to leer.

As Sir John Suckling (the most aptly named dirty old man in history—or one who would have been so if he hadn't foolishly decided to die at thirty-three) said three and a half centuries ago, with amazing prescience:

> Her legs beneath her miniskirt,
> Like pulsing shafts, strode in and out,
> And glistened in the light.

Hot pants, which, superficially, seem to exhibit to the free gaze all the areas that the miniskirts have are, nevertheless, a poorer stimulus to leering. Research into the matter is at present proceeding and I shall perhaps have something more to say here in the second edition of this scholarly work.

Pantyhose, on the other hand, although covering acres of bare skin, are excellent subjects for the leer. Again, experts are divided on the reasons.

NEW

POINTS

AT WHICH

TO LEER

THERE ARE ADVANCES IN LEERING, THESE DAYS, as in other technical achievements. The leer that was suitable ten years ago will not do today, while leers now exist that were unheard of a decade earlier. Let us consider a bit of little-known history in this connection.

Sometime during the 1930's, women, having stripped off enough layers of frontal textile, discovered that insufficient material was left to protect the delicate tissues of the bosom. To protect these, modern engineering devised a structure that served to compress the bosom into firm cone-shaped objects which, far from requiring protection, could allow unlimited maneuver without danger. Unavoidably it caught the masculine eye—or some other part of the male anatomy if he weren't careful, leaving a nasty bruise.

The service performed to womankind by this new garment can not easily be exaggerated. It was first designed by an organization of bioengineers who, although individually anonymous, have become world-famous by the corporate title of "Bosom-Rehabilitation Associates." The garment they engineered possessing the small initials BRA on the strap quickly became known, in consequence, as the "bra."

The gentlemen of B.R.A. carefully labored to give each woman that firmly jutting profile one would naturally associate with strength of will and character, and it worked. Many is the woman who, in her natural unprotected state, would have slunk into a room, abashed and uncertain, but who, with her bra firmly in place, could walk in, shoulders back and chest thrown out, proudly aware that every man in the place would at once note and admire her strength of character.

Every woman felt uplifted by the experience so

B. R. A. ASSOCIATES

that the industry began to speak of the "uplift bra."

And yet the uplift bra had its troubles. For one thing, the designers had unaccountably placed its hooks in the back. In addition, the straps cut the shoulders and in hot weather there were such matters as heat, perspiration and skin rashes.

Little by little the thought came that it might be possible to eliminate the bra and allow the contents to find their natural level, or, as President Nixon so succinctly put it in discussing this very problem, the time had come for America to adopt a lower profile.

Certain of the more excitable women determined not merely to eliminate the bra but to burn it as a gesture of contempt. The slogan arose: "Let's Ignite Bras." This was abbreviated to L.I.B. and in no time at all "Women's Lib" was a power in the land.

The result was, in the light of hindsight, inevitable. The ladies found themselves back where they were in the 1930's and, indeed, worse off than ever. The sturdier fabrics of a much earlier day, the taffeta dress and corduroy blouse, had given way to sheer synthetics. What had earlier been hidden and protected by the bra was hidden and protected no longer by virtually anything. Indeed, the tender caress of the soft synthetic irritated the delicate bosom surface till every unevenness was accentuated and softly revealed.

At a time when President Nixon was making one point very, very clear, the average young girl on the streets of New York was doing exactly twice as well.

And dirty old men, on those same streets, found that they had a new target—and new hazards. Without the constriction of the bra, the average young lady, moving forward in a healthy free-swinging stride, presents what can only be described as a moving target.

It is therefore difficult for the dirty old man to get to the point; for the point shifts. It moves wildly at the slightest bodily motion. It jiggles, wobbles and dangles; heaves, yaws and rolls; vibrates, oscillates and undulates.

The dirty old man may find himself trying to follow every movement by use of eye muscles, head muscles or both. This is not advisable. Aside from the fact that in the attempt to concentrate too entirely on the target, he may walk into a wall, the constant movement of eyes or head or both will induce dizziness, headache, nausea and even that dread affliction of the inveterate leerer, watering eyes. The whole complex of symptoms makes up the syndrome of "mammamobilism."

Mammamobilism is known to the medical profession by the euphemistic phrase, "nipple shock," but in this book I have no use for euphemisms and do not intend to employ them. The general public, the taxi driver, the construction worker, everyone, says "mammamobilism" and that's what I shall say, too.

The Italians, far wiser than we in their attitude toward sex, have no compunctions about using the phrase. You will recall that in the great opera *Rigoletto* the Duke, on the occasion when Gilda runs past him, jiggling, claps his hand to his brow and begins the brilliant tenor aria: "Oh, mammamobile—"

Although you can see that the disease played so important a part in the opera written by Joe

---

Green* a century and a quarter ago, thanks to the extraordinary equipment of the pasta-consuming coloratura soprano of his day, it did not strike the American public till just a few short years ago. Mammamobolism is not amenable to penicillin or to any of the other antibiotics. Prevention, then, is the key. Do *not* try to follow the moving target. Fix the eye rather upon some key portion of the dress pattern and allow the sense of sight to be titillated sporadically.

*Green, having emigrated to Italy, adopted the Italian version of his name, Giuseppe Verdi. For reasons known only to opera buffs, the Italian name is actually better known today than the name he was born with in Poughkeepsie, New York.

GIUSEPPE VERDI

AT
WHOM
TO
LEER

WHEN THERE IS BUT ONE WOMAN IN VIEW, THE problem of whom to leer at is relatively simple. With the alternative of leering at a woman or at empty air, the average dirty old man will usually choose to leer at the woman. Almost instinctively, once he has developed the principle of sensuousness, he will realize that empty air offers little in the way of reward.

Or as Shakespeare said, in one of his more profound penetrations of the human condition:

Nothing will come of nothing.*

*It may occur to the less desirable class of readers of this book that I am making up the quotations. Not so, for I am a man of the most exalted integrity. If you think this quotation is too profound even for Shakespeare, you may look it up. You will find it in Act I, scene i, line 92 of—what else—"King Leer."

The problem really arises when more than one woman is in view. The question then is on whom to bestow one's attentions. The natural tendency, perhaps, is to choose the one who is youngest, prettiest, barest, or unstraightest—or some combination of these.

Nonsense! That is the young man's reaction; the greenhorn's; the know-nothing's.

The sensuous dirty old man knows better. He leers at all indiscriminately, for each variety and subspecies of the feminine gender has its own kind of response and there is something rewarding in each kind. The young girl may respond with simpers and wriggles that will hold you rapt with their charm, but the older girl is more deeply grateful, and gratitude, you know, is not to be sneered at.

It may be impossible, as the poet and dendrophile, Joyce Kilmer, said in 1913, for a man to make a tree, but a grateful woman offers less difficulty. There is every reason to suppose, Joyce Kilmer aside, that no man, given his free choice, would try to make a tree anyway.

The ancient Greeks felt that trees, particularly oak trees, contained beautiful young female creatures called dryads, but there is every reason to think the ancient Greeks were drunk at the time.*

Indeed, the deplorable business of picking and choosing the target of the leer is what, more than anything else, has given dirty old men a bad name. Innumerable surveys have made it quite clear that when a respectable elderly man makes up to a giggling young lady, it is not the giggling young lady so accosted that is offended by the action, but rather the granite-faced dowager, standing unnoticed by her side, who is. It is she who makes derogatory remarks concerning dirty old men, and is quite likely to attack him with an umbrella.

This phenomenon was well known to the ancient sages and poets. King William III of Great Britain, for instance, who wasn't interested in his wife, and who suffered the consequences, improvised a

*Don't get me wrong. I'm not implying the Greeks would believe anything. The Greek princess, Danae, wound up one morning unexpectedly pregnant. Her father, Acrisius, naturally inquired as to the fellow's name, with the notion, one would imagine, of instituting a suit for child-support. Danae said, "I was just sitting there minding my own business, Dad, when the god, Zeus, appeared to me in the form of a shower of gold—" After that, Acrisius put Danae in a leaky boat and shoved it out to sea, which is what any decent father would do if his one and only tried to tell him a whopper like that.

very well-known couplet once, when he was in conversation with the dramatist, William Congreve. It went:

> Heaven has no rage like beauty unexplored,
> Nor Hell a fury like a dame ignored.*

Rudyard Kipling put it even more succinctly, when he said:

> When the dirty older fellow gives the
>   younger girl a miss,
>   She will sob into her hankie and will
>   often softly hiss,
> But the older doll so treated rends the
>   peasant tooth and nail,
>   For the ancient dame neglected is quite
>   deadly to the male.

I think it is scarcely necessary to warn the dirty old man to concentrate rather on the bleaker of the two prospects before him if he wishes to re-

*Congreve put this couplet into a play he wrote in 1697 but got it all wrong.

RUDYARD KIPLING

main in one piece. Time enough to pass on to the more luscious morsel when the ancient target has been reduced to a hoarse, girlish giggle. *Verbum sap.**

*This is from a Latin phrase which, translated literally, means "Anyone who needs to be told this in words is a thoroughgoing sap."

THE

TOUCH

THE EYE, ALTHOUGH THE MOST IMPORTANT OF THE sense organs, is not the most intimate. For one thing, sight is essentially long-distance. The naked eye can make out the Andromeda galaxy as a dim, cloudy patch and it is over two million light-years away. This can be brought down to the normal standards of measurement of the dirty old man by converting it into city blocks. The Andromeda galaxy is 200,000,000,000,000,000,000,000 city blocks away. This is a sizable distance; spy a girl 200,000,-000,000,000,000,000 city blocks away and it is scarcely worthwhile walking toward her.

Clothe the naked eye with a good telescope and objects can be made out that are up to four thousand times as far away as the Andromeda galaxy and even astronomers admit that this is going too far. Raquel Welch, at the distance of even the nearest quasar (about 100,000,000,000,000,000,-000,000 city blocks away) can stay there for all I care. And I think I can say without fear of successful contradiction that the entire staff at Mt. Palomar Observatory would agree with me.

What's more, sight grows inefficient at just those distances that are most interesting. Objects within a foot of one's nose grow fuzzy and there is difficulty focussing. The eyes must cross uncomfortably and painfully. Indeed, some maintain that it was with reference to a situation such as this that Swift made his famous remark (referred to earlier in this book) concerning "a sight for sore eyes."

Touch is quite another thing. For touch there must be contact. Though you stretch your body, arms and legs as far as ever you can, yet the object contacted cannot be more than a few feet

---

from your center of gravity. Furthermore, while touch with fingertips and tongue is most sensitive, it can be carried on with any part of the body. The closer the object contacted, then, the more efficient and widespread the touch.

The question then is not whether or not a girl should be touched. The question is merely where, when and how she should be touched.

The word has gone out that in Italy, young men perform a ritual compression of the plumper portion of the left buttock (or the right, if they are left-handed) between thumb and forefinger. As a result, American women of maturer age tramp the streets of Rome and Naples endlessly, looking for young men in an ardent desire to quench their natural curiosity. This is particularly true, I am told, of the American gradeschool teacher who, in a laudable desire to return with an accurate report of foreign customs to her small charges, leaves no doorway unexplored.

As a result the young men, with calloused fingers and aching tendons, have set up lookouts. When the report is signaled as to the approach of a prim and austere female of American aspect, with eyes glinting through rimless spectacles and nostrils flaring, they all speed into hideouts.

Clearly, if the muscularity of bottom-pinching wears out the virile young Neapolitan, the dirty old man should have nothing to do with it. Not only is it painful to the fingers; it is gross and unsubtle.

Remember that the touch, ideally, should bespeak affection. The arm protectively upon the shoulder, or slipped gently about the waist, is what is wanted and needed by the women of today. There is the fond chuck under the chin, the gentle tweak of the cheek, the fatherly pat of the hand—

In the face of small intimate gestures of this kind, the lady involved will glow and expand. So, very likely, will you.

Of course, the average old man may fear to make the plunge into touchery. There is nothing so pathetic as the sight of some old gentleman, trembling with the fear of being called a "toucherous old man," shuffling about and hesitating to pat the rosy cheek of a young lady who is aching for the reassurance such a gesture will bring her.

The sensuous dirty old man does not make this mistake but keeps firmly in mind the verse of that doughty warrior, James Graham, 1st Marquess of Montrose:

> He either fears his fate too much
> Or his deserts are small,
>
> That dares not put it to that touch
> That makes the maiden fall.

It is the essence of the touch, of course, that there is a certain fuzziness about it, both in time and space. An arm about the shoulder or waist need not be instantly removed; to do so might even be construed as an insult.

There is the case of a lady I know, for instance, who noted that, during a moment of passionate political argument at the dinner table, the left hand of the man on her immediate right (who was avidly supporting one of those controversial post office reform programs that divide friends and families into warring factions) came unwittingly to rest upon her own right knee. As nearly as she can recall the moment, it was when he was demonstrating the speed with which letters might reach their destination under certain conditions that his left hand, overshooting its mark, landed on her knee. Had the tablecloth not hidden the entire operation, she is convinced the gentleman would have noticed his mistake.

The young lady in question waited a polite interval for the mistake to be corrected. When it was not, she fixed her neighbor with a haughty stare and whispered freezingly, "Sir, you are taking an unendurable liberty. If you do not remove your hand from my knee within half an hour, I shall scream."

It was no more than fifteen minutes, you can be sure, before the gentleman had removed his hand in some confusion.

And yet he betrayed his ignorance and gaucherie in the manner in which he did it. For having delayed in the first place, he took his hand entirely away. The sensuous dirty old man would have known better. At the first indication that the lady was not satisfied to have her knee gently and therapeutically warmed by manual contact, he would have removed it upward and clasped the thigh instead. A lady is entitled to have her knee free if she feels that her thigh would feel more grateful for the warmth.

The sensuous dirty old man has learned the final art of the touch, that of making it so gentle and innocent that the young lady involved can scarcely believe it is happening and therefore ignores it. This presents an exercise in innocence both on the part of the toucher and touchee that should bring tears of envy to all beholders.

I have seen many a dirty old man with an arm that began at the lady's waist, shifted by such slow and gentle degrees as to pass eventually through the warmth of the armpit to the budding softness of the maidenly bosom, without that shift ever being noticed by the young lady. At least, she gave no signs of noticing.

It is this cultivated unawareness that is the hallmark of the well-brought-up young lady, the ability to not-notice the gentle and intermittent pressure of knee against thigh that will make you able

WALTER SAVAGE LANDOR

to say with the poet, Walter Savage Landor:*

> A night of memories and of thighs
> I consecrate to thee.

*Landor's most famous line was "Nature I loved; and next to Nature, Art." No biographer has yet determined who Arthur was. Both loves seem to have been unreciprocated and Landor so often expressed his savage sentiments over this that his friends began to regard "savage" as his middle name.

SPEECH

SO FAR I HAVE TALKED ONLY ABOUT EXPRESSIONS, actions and, at best, inchoate sounds. These are important, but they are to the total equipment of the sensuous dirty old man as silent movies are to the talkies.

Speech is the crown of the sensuous dirty old man's art. While there is a certain amount of communication in a sigh, a deal of significance in the wiggling eyebrow, a clarity of expression in the sharp stare, enormous admiration in the involuntary ejaculation—there is still nothing like the English language for delivering carefully-thought-out and subtle feelings.

Unless you are French, of course, in which case the French language may be used.

Many a dirty old man, however, shies away from saying anything. It may be that he has read too many Victorian novels—novels in which the hero says to the young lady, "Cynthia, may—may I hope?" and in which Cynthia then draws herself up to her full height, poniards him with a sharp glance and says, "Sir! Your speech is too free. Have a care, for I am a pure woman."

Whether Cynthia is, or is not, that contradiction in terms, a pure woman, is here beside the point. In the United States, it is illegal for Cynthia to express herself in this fashion, for the dirty old man is specifically protected by our glorious Constitution. In the very first amendment of the Bill of Rights it is stated, "Congress shall make no law . . . abridging the freedom of speech." Look it up if you don't believe me.

In other words, no matter how Cynthia may protest, it is your legal and inalienable right to speak freely to her.

What's more, we can go further. Not only is it possible to speak freely to her, but you can enfold

---

her in your arms and hold her tightly while murmuring your endearments in her ear, since the same glorious amendment to our glorious Constitution adds to the above quoted phrase ". . . or of the press."

So press away, boys. It is your right and duty as free Americans to demonstrate to the rest of the world, downtrodden as they are under oppression and sunken in misery, just how proud we are of the United States and of its free institutions.

(There are some radicals who hold that this same glorious amendment also permits orgies. The amendment goes on to forbid any abridgement by Congress of "the right of the people peaceably to assemble." The radicals insist that there is nowhere that the art of peace is more assiduously maintained by assembly than in an orgy. However, there are cogent arguments on the other side, too, and a decision by the Supreme Court will probably be necessary, sooner or later, in this sensitive area.)

WHAT

TO

SAY

GIVEN THE RIGHT TO SPEAK FREELY, WHAT DOES one say to a young lady or, for that matter, to a woman of maturer charms, who is a complete stranger or whom one has met only casually.

Naturally this varies with the speaker and each dirty old man has the right and the privilege of inventing his own method of oral attack. It is here that dirty old mannishness can be at its most creative.

You must understand that it is useless for one dirty old man to consult another in an effort to pick up effective lines, for what will suit one will not suit another. Remember—it is your own style that is best for you; to attempt to memorize another's words or intonations will do you no good, for you cannot deliver the offspring of another's style with any convincing authority.

Nevertheless, a few rules can be advanced, and a few examples offered as stimuli, if not as models.

First, do not make a bald and unadorned suggestion concerning some improper action. The woman, however much she may approve, will feel impelled, out of a sense of honor, to express a reluctant refusal on the grounds that the subway is too crowded at the moment, or that the sidewalk is too cold. Trivial points, perhaps, but such excuses and others equally unimportant have been made in response to invitations that lack finesse.

Worse still, the woman concerned may agree enthusiastically and it may then occur to *you* that the subway is too crowded or the sidewalk too cold, and you may find it difficult to back out without embarrassment.

No! The young lady must be led onward gracefully, while you yourself must remember to be always polite and complimentary.

I know a man, for instance, who on meeting a woman of striking structure and notable décolletage, says, "May I speak to you confidentially a moment, dear madam?"

The woman does not live who has ever refused to listen to something confidential. She inclines her pretty ear. The man in question, leaning close, says slowly, "I have nothing really to say, dear madam, except to remark that the view is magnificent."

This is the suavity of the truly sensuous dirty old man. Consider that the woman, in dressing for the occasion, must have wondered, as she viewed herself at various angles before the mirror, as to whether the view were *really* magnificent. She may have had misgivings on the subject—and now she is reassured by a man of maturity, who may be expected to have considerable experience along these particular points, that it is.

It is no wonder that at this point her breath is very likely to quicken with delight and her fair bosom heave with the tumultuous passions surging within her—which of course makes the view even more magnificent.

In fact, even if the view is *not* magnificent, it is only right to say it is.

This, of course, brings up the question of whether it is proper to lie in these delicate matters. Should the sensuous dirty old man stoop so low? Does not the ancient Greek dramatist, Sophocles, say,

> Truly, to tell lies is not honorable.

And would Sophocles steer you wrong?

Let us not, however, take passages of the great thinkers out of context. Sophocles goes on to say,

> But when the truth entails tremendous ruin
> To speak dishonorably is pardonable.

All right, then. Picture yourself bending over a lady, when it is suddenly borne in on you that size, proportion and delicacy are all wanting. Should you then say, "My dear madam, the view is far short of magnificent. It is, in fact, nauseating."

The result will entail tremendous ruin, unless you are the kind who can coldly view the anguish

SOPHOCLES

and tears of a brokenhearted female, who is sys-tematically and savagely beating you up.

The French, who lead the world in the dirty-hood of old men, have a saying, "Noblesse oblige." This is frequently mistranslated by those who do not realize it is a shortened form of "Non blessé, oblige," which means, literally, "Not wounded, oblige" or, at greater length, "If you don't oblige a lady, she is going to wound you badly." French ladies are, of course, more likely to use the heel of the shoe in casual remonstrance, and generally have longer and sharper heels than American women do,* but I think the rule is a general one.

It also delights a lady when you use her own phrases as a take-off point. This allows an ex-change which covers all concerned with an appear-ance of wit to the delight of the young woman.

Let us imagine the following circumstance, which frequently arises. You have complimented a woman on the fetching color of her bra, a corner of which you have glimpsed, of (if she is wearing a miniskirt, and has seated herself with abandon at a

---

*Frenchman, I am told, tend to *be* bigger heels than American men, so perhaps this is only fair.

time when you are suitably alert) on the clever match of the pattern of her nethergarment with that of her dress—or else on her courage in not wearing a bra or, possibly, a nethergarment.

In response to your warm admiration she is very likely to giggle and say, "Oh, you have made my day."

It is then the work of a moment to say gallantly, "Your day, my dear young miss [or reverend madam] is not what I am trying to make."

Here is another example—

The other day a gentleman of mature years had occasion to ask of a generously endowed young lady in an office where she was working the gift of a paper clip. She offered him a large paper clip.

"That's too big," he said.

"I only have big ones," said the dear young thing.

"So I noticed," said the dirty old man, to universal applause.

This, the dirty old man assured me, was not planned in advance, and I cannot stress the importance of seizing the occasion without hesitation. The unexpected thrust is bound to create a stir and the whisper will go from girl to girl, "Oh, what a clever fellow. Isn't he sexy?" and who could ask for more.*

Indeed, the climax of the dirty old man's wit is to have a young lady say to him, "Oh, I can't say *anything* to you."

Obviously, it is a source of inexpressible comfort to any woman to know that she need not strain for effect, that she need not work hard to achieve a passionate response—that *anything* she says will elicit what is wanted and needed.

Let us suppose, for instance, that the paper clip incident had taken place with a green, young man —handsome, tanned, muscular and with a charming smile—in short, possessing none of the attributes likely to attract a lady with taste.

He asks for a paper clip and the secretary says, with a meaningful simper, "I only have big ones."

"Too bad," he says, like the oaf he is. "Can't use them."

---

*To young ladies of any age, a clever fellow seems sexy. What's more, a sexy fellow seems clever. To the male, this is "arguing in a circle"; to a female, this is "self-evident logic." Need I say that it profits a dirty old man to adhere strictly to feminine lines of thought, if he expects ever to adhere to anything else feminine?

There is nothing left for the poor young lady to do but flee to the surgeon. No wonder she turns for relief and comfort to the dirty old man, who would never fail her in such a case.

Remember that even the most casual of compliments can be given that extra little touch that women adore.

Any fool can see a woman in a new dress (or even an old one) and say, "Good heavens, what a magnificent dress!"

If he leaves it there, it is the kind of routine remark that an unfledged youth might say—pleasant, but lacking the true tang of the stately compliment that only age and experience can deliver.

The dirty old man would say, "Good heavens, what a magnificent dress," then, after a pause, add with a note of awe, "Or am I merely judging by the contents?"

No woman of flesh and blood could resist that. I am told by one practitioner that he made this precise remark to a spinster of seventy-five winters, who then blushed, wriggled and giggled like a girl in response. Undoubtedly the improvement in her circulation, though temporary, may have added hours, or even days, to her life, and the good deed was carefully recorded to the credit of the dirty old man in the books of heaven.

The dirty old man should hold himself ready at all times and under even the most untoward circumstances to express gallantry. I have recorded the case, for instance, of the dirty old man who seated himself wearily in an empty chair in an office while waiting to see someone.

A young lady entered and said, in a sharp, unfriendly manner, "That's my chair you're sitting on."

At which the dirty old man replied, without rising, "Merely endeavoring, my dear young lady, to absorb the pleasant lingering warmth that your ravishing rear has left upon this otherwise cold and uninviting chair."

The young lady not only permitted him to keep the seat—she brought him a cup of coffee as well.

—But the "buttock-swapping effect" is a graduate study which cannot be dealt with adequately in a basic primer such as this one. Let us pass on.

ORGIES

I HAVE MENTIONED ORGIES BEFORE, AS POSSIBLY having been guaranteed by the Constitution. In our more permissive society of today, such matters are coming under more and more earnest discussion, so it is only fitting that I consider the matter here.

Let me first state that one dirty old man plus more than one woman is *not* an orgy in any sense of the word. A dirty old man, if sufficiently sensuous, can admire, leer, pat and intimately compliment any number of women. The dear things will eagerly vie for his attentions, and will feel a warm sisterhood among themselves at finding themselves in a noncompetitive situation.

It is the young man who picks and chooses, who flatters one and ignores many, who rouses feelings of envy and hatred in the soft bosoms of the rejected, and, what is worse, encourages the (perhaps) firmer bosom of the accepted to feel pride and disdain.

Not so with the dirty old man, whose efforts are always in the direction of peace with comfort.

It is when *more* than one dirty old man is involved, regardless of the number of women, that the affair becomes an orgy.

There are some experts who affect to believe that there are advantages to an orgy. They argue that if one dirty old man is at a loss for a proper comment, the other may not be. If one dirty old man is, for the moment, carrying the brunt of keeping a large number of women happy, he may be relieved at being able to assign a certain number of them to the ministrations of another.

And yet, to me, it seems that the arguments against the orgy are overwhelming. It is not to be denied that to one dirty old man, another dirty old man often seems crude and vile. Indeed, I have been present on a number of occasions in which each of a pair of dirty old men thought the other crude and vile.

It has been suggested that when pluralism is involved, the two or more dirty old men who are acting in tandem should be close and intimate friends. In that case, you, for instance, will be better able to forgive the other (or others) their crudeness and vilehood.

Perhaps so, but this is not the most delicate portion of the difficulty. It is almost inevitable that your friend, no matter how close he may be to you ordinarily, will totally fail to appreciate the suavity and gallantry of your own approach and may mutter something about your being "crude and vile" under his breath. This demonstration of poor taste is next to impossible to forgive.

Is it worth it, then? Some modern souls claim to see in the orgy a chance for the spirit to expand in great freedom; a chance to display unselfishness and a spirit of nonpossessiveness which they say is badly needed in the modern world. I cannot deny the selfless altruism implicit in this viewpoint. Balancing that, however, is the selfless urge to spare the ladies the crudehood and vilicity of lesser men.

To put it in a nutshell, the spirit of unselfishness can be argued in two directions. One might selflessly argue the rights of one's fellow-dirty-old-men to share women equally with oneself. One might also selflessly argue the rights of women to be free of the lesser attempts of lesser men and to bathe entirely in the superior ambience of oneself.

I think it is more important to think of the rights of ladies than of men, and with that in mind, I fight off all other dirty old men. As Thomas Babington, Lord Macaulay, put it in his moving verse on the subject:

> For how can man do better
>   Than, facing fearful odds
> For the welfare of the ladies,
>   To beat off all the clods.

And you can bet Lord Macaulay knew about such things. This very passage comes from a collection of his poems known as *Lays of Ancient Rome* and Ancient Rome had some darned good ones.

So do as you wish, my friends, but I adhere to the good old-fashioned virtues, and prefer to keep my dozen or so ladies to myself. Orgies are for weaklings.

PROBLEMS

THERE ARE MOMENTS OF EMBARRASSMENT THAT all of us encounter. Many a correspondent, hoping to take advantage of my virtuosity in the field, has written me letters of inquiry, and I will take the opportunity here of dealing with them.

Actually, the questions are only three in number, when you get down to basics. Though the problems seem infinite, they will always shake down to one of the following three situations, or possibly to a combination of them.

First: What if the lady involved gets angry?

This is an improper question. The lady never gets angry.

What does happen is that the dirty old man may get maladroit.

If you are clumsy, ill-timed or offensive, would it not stand to reason that the lady would be annoyed? Wouldn't you?

On those occasions, ask yourself what you have done wrong. Reread this book. Buy a second copy, perhaps, in case the first was improperly bound and reread that.

I remember, in this connection, what I was once told by an eminent practitioner in the field. He was asked the proper grammatical way of expressing illness.

He answered, "The most elegant way is to say 'I feel ill,' but 'I feel bad' is perhaps acceptable."

His questioner said, "What about 'I feel badly.' "

At this the eminent practitioner, with an expression of revulsion, said, "The only one with a right to say 'I feel badly' is in inept dirty old man."

I have treasured that remark. Or as a Chinese sage once said: "Surely, it is written in letters of gold on a wall of jade that if one would never feel badly one would never feel bad."

Second: What if a husband or boyfriend shows up?

The incorrect thing to do is to spring away as though one had done wrong, or to make a vague pretense of having done nothing at all. The disappointed and hurt expression on the girl's face, as you suddenly show, in the most callous possible manner, that you don't think enough of her to risk a broken arm, will naturally enrage the husband. After all, it's enough for him that *he* doesn't think so; it is perfectly infuriating to suppose that even strangers don't.

The obvious thing to do is to look up when one hears the rough and rasping breath of the outraged male-proprietor, smile and say: "Ah, is this the gentleman with the remarkably good taste to have married [to be affianced to] [to be interested in] this utterly charming young lady that I now have the pleasure of meeting?"

Or, if you have actually been interrupted at the moment when, in full fatherly flow, you have been caressing an arm or another portion of the anatomy, you may say, "I have taken the liberty, as an expert in such matters, of inspecting the arm [the leg] [the clavicle] of this fascinating young creature and I wish to assure you that you have made an extraordinarily good choice here. Prime quality, my good sir, prime quality."

Expressions of this sort are not only most gratifying to the woman involved who, ten to one, has been distractedly attempting to convince the proprietary man in question that she is indeed prime quality and who has been fighting a losing battle in this respect.

It will also impress the man with the extraordinary quality of his own good taste, something of which he may have begun to have sickening doubts recently.

Then, too, even if nothing on earth could convince him that the girl of his heart is of any value, your extraordinary praise will puzzle and confuse him long enough to enable you to beat a safe retreat.

A retreat *is* recommended, even when the husband or boyfriend is a miserable little shnook whom you can easily manhandle, or a placid fellow who seems uninterested in the whole thing.

Many a dirty old man, on being interrupted by

the husband, has been overly slow in retreating and has had the painful experience of listening to the husband say, with emotions varying from indifference to eagerness, "Listen, if you want her, take her."

Not only does this, nine times out of ten, lead to a family altercation that is unpleasant for any outsider to have to listen to, but it is quite possible for the woman involved to turn to you and say, "All right, dear, you just take me and we'll show this klutz, won't we?"

This is a situation in which no good answer exists. All possible alternatives lead to destruction.

Third: What if you, as a sensuous dirty old man, happen to be married and your wife—

But this question is unnecessary to complete, particularly since the very thought is so painful.

The best advice is not to be caught. There was once a time when a dirty old man, could, as a matter of common prudence, choose those moments when his wife was in another city, and only then would he conduct his operations. These days, though, with jet flight so common and with planes taking on passengers indiscriminately, one can rely on nothing.

Attempts can be made, of course, to patch over matters, if only because there is something gallant about the man who goes down fighting. You can drop the arm you are holding, not suddenly as though you have been caught in guilty confusion (though you have), but judiciously as though weighing matters, and, turning to your wife, you can say, "On the whole, my dear, it falls far short of the qualities I have grown accustomed to in you —as I have just been telling this elderly woman."

Naturally, this must be done with the greatest possible delicacy, for danger threatens, as I scarcely need tell you, from two directions.

I once knew a dirty old man who, operating along these lines went too far, in his enthusiasm, and just as he was on the point of completely mollifying his wife was thoroughly eradicated by the outraged purse of the other lady.

Shakespeare puts this situation well, I think, when in "The Merchant of Venice" he says: "Thus when I shun Scylla, your father, I fall into Charybdis, your mother."*

*Scylla and Charybdis are to be found in Homer's great second epic, along with many other odd names, people and events, which is why it is called the "Odyssey."

THE
ULTIMATE

BUT LET US, IN CLOSING, PASS ON TO THE MOST dangerous problem of all—the ultimate.

Every once in a while, a dirty old man, practicing his profession as best he can, meets that dread adversary, the dirty old woman.

Dirty old women come in all ages, shapes and sizes, so there is no certain way of recognizing them in advance. The chance of being caught *always* exists.

What's more, one ought to know the worst about dirty old women. They are not suave, neither are they subtle. They do not believe in wasting time. They are harsh and determined and have an eye like a hawk.

And so it is that every once in a while, when a dirty old man casually places his arm about a feminine waist and says, "Oh, my little rose-breasted nuthatch—" he suddenly recognizes his doom has come. The little dove turns out to be an osprey after all, the little rabbit a wolverine—and the dirty old man knows there is no escape.

Flipping her cigarette away, the dirty old woman turns on him with her face unpleasantly contorted into passionate glee and says, hoarsely, "Right on, bud. Let's go."

Do not think for a moment there is any escape. If you attempt ignominious flight, she will callously trip you up and stand on you while lighting another cigarette.

If you tremble and cry in the hope of evoking pity, she will tuck you under her arm and walk off with you.

If you attempt hauteur and, drawing yourself up coldly, say, "Madame, you mistake me; I am not that kind of dirty old man," she will get you in the guts with the sharp point of her umbrella (or her elbow, whichever is harder).

Nothing will work.

There is only one alternative. We must face the issue with hard firmness and resolutely prepare for the encounter.

We must remember the wise words of Winston Churchill who, speaking on a very similar occasion, said to Lady Astor (and I quote from memory):

"Let us therefore brace ourselves to our duties, and so bear ourselves that though the occasion seem to last for a thousand years, yet you will finally be forced to look up and say, 'Oh, my, you really *are* a dirty old man.' "

And with that, I leave you. —Good hunting!

SIR WINSTON CHURCHILL

SPECIAL NOTE

It is quite possible that many a thoughtful reader, having finished this book, has points concerning which additional information is required.

The author, motivated by concern for suffering humanity, will endeavor to help. All mail should be addressed care of the publisher.

WALKER & CO.
720 Fifth Ave.
N.Y.C., N.Y. 10019

Other SIGNET Titles You Will Enjoy

☐ **ADVICE TO MEN by Robert Chartham.** Avoiding stereo-
typed patterns of sexual practice and sweeping away the
puritanical cobwebs of inhibition, Robert Chartham shows
how lovers of all ages can keep their lovemaking con-
tinually fresh and exciting. (#Q5075—95¢)

☐ **ADVICE TO WOMEN by Robert Chartham.** A sensitive and
enlightening manual that liberates women from such
Victorian hang-ups as modesty and shame.
(#Q5076—95¢)

☐ **THE STUD by Jackie Collins.** A novel about the ambi-
tious, fast living—and loving—people among the swinging
"in-crowd" of London's discothéque scene . . . and Tony
Burg, ex-waiter, ex-nothing—now elevated to the rank of
superstud. (#Q4609—95¢)

☐ **ROYAL FLASH by George MacDonald Fraser.** A new and
crackling episode in the tremendously entertaining ad-
ventures of England's #1 scoundrel, that bully, liar and
womanizing scoundrel named Flashman. ". . . hilariously
funny . . ."—**New York Times Book Review**
(#Y4831—$1.25)

Humor Titles from SIGNET

☐ **IT'S HARD TO BE HIP AFTER THIRTY by Judith Viorst.** What happens after the glamour wears off in a marriage. Mrs. Viorst tells us in her funny, moving poems.
(#Y4124—$1.25)

☐ **AM I TOO HEAVY DEAR? by W. H. Manville and James Wright.** What this uproarious book of cartoons is all about is sex. Here to our vast amusement are the embarrassing words, the all-too-familiar emotions, everything we thought wild and passionate back there in the moonbeams.
(#P4103—60¢)

☐ **DEAR DATING COMUPTER edited by Bill Adler.** One of the foremost collectors and connoisseurs of modern day humor has put together a wildly original book about the matches and mis-matches that computer dating has arranged.
(#T4247—75¢)

☐ **THE NEUROTIC'S NOTEBOOK by Mignon McLaughlin.** A totally fresh volume that examines the neurotic and his characteristics. Men, love, women and life are well "covered" in this funny book.
(#P4266—60¢)